Our Lady of Guadalupe

Also in this Series
Saint Francis of Assisi
Saint Teresa of Avila
Saint Michael the Archangel
Hildegard of Bingen
Saint John of the Cross

DEVOTIONS, PRAYERS & LIVING WISDOM

Our Lady of Guadalupe

Edited by Mirabai Starr

Sounds True, Inc., Boulder, CO 80306

© 2008 Mirabai Starr

SOUNDS TRUE is a trademark of Sounds True, Inc. All rights reserved. No part of this book may be used or reproduced in any manner without written permission from the author and publisher.

Book designed by Lisa Kerans

Published 2008
Printed in Canada
ISBN 978-1-59179-795-1

Library of Congress Cataloging-in-Publication Data
Starr, Mirabai.
  Our Lady of Guadalupe : devotions, prayers, and living wisdom / Mirabai Starr.
  p. cm.—(Devotions, prayers, and living wisdom series ; bk. five)
ISBN 978-1-59179-795-1 (hardcover)
1. Mary, Blessed Virgin, Saint—Prayers and devotions.
2. Mary, Blessed Virgin, Saint—Devotion to—Mexico
3. Guadalupe, Our Lady of. I. Title.

BT660.G8S83 2008
242'.74—dc22

2007042895

For a free catalog of wisdom teachings for the inner life, call (800) 333-9185 or visit www.soundstrue.com.

Contents

Publisher's Note / vii

Editor's Note / ix

Opening Prayer / xiii

Introduction / 1

Chapter One:
    She Appears / 19

Chapter Two:
    Blossoms of Mercy / 49

Chapter Three:
    Mother of the People / 83

Closing Prayer / 107

Sources / 113

Bibliography / 117

Credits / 119

About Sounds True / 122

Publisher's Note

Sounds True's *Devotions, Prayers, and Living Wisdom* series began with a desire to offer the essential teachings of great saints, mystics, and spiritual figures in a format that is compatible with meditation and contemplation. Each book contains poems, prayers, songs, and prose written by or in veneration of a figure who has transcended human confusion, and whose wisdom might awaken our own. It is our hope that these books will offer you insight, renewal, and companionship on the spiritual path.

Editor's Note

Our Lady of Guadalupe is ubiquitous in my homeland of New Mexico and in the heartland of Mexico, where my family spends a great deal of time. While I was born a Jew and have maintained a long-time Buddhist meditation practice, I have always identified with this particular representation of the Divine Mother and have taken comfort in surrounding myself with carved and painted reminders of her. Now, having immersed myself in the stories and teachings surrounding the miraculous apparition of *La Virgen Maria* for this book, I feel I have uncovered the secret life of an old friend, and I love her more deeply than ever.

Because Our Lady of Guadalupe did not live in a physical body and therefore did not leave writings of her own, I have drawn on prayers and poems written to her, as well as accounts written about her, including passages from the *Nican Mopohua,* which conveys the words she is said to have spoken when she first appeared to the Aztec peasant Juan Diego on Tepeyac Hill on December 12, 1531. Readers can find a detailed source list at the back of the book.

The text is organized into three chapters, reflecting three major themes I find arising in the Guadalupe materials: the miracle of the apparition; mercy and compassion; and social justice. Each chapter opens and closes with a reflection of my own, distinguished by italics, which serves as a contemporary meditation on the theme of that chapter.

It is my deep hope that in these pages you, too, will either discover or deepen your personal relationship with this great being who reflects the feminine face of the Divine. May Our Lady of Guadalupe guide you on your path home to your sacred self.

I am deeply grateful for the generous contributions and wise council of Professor Tom Shaw, Professor Larry Torres, Father David Denny, Father William Hart McNichols, Demetria Martinez, Arnulfo and

Juanita Mendoza, Kaysi Contreras, Sarah Jane Freymann, Kelly Notaras, Haven Iverson, and Rose Marie Berger.

— Mirabai Starr
August 2007

Opening Prayer

Praise to you,
Our Lady of Guadalupe,
who appeared to a humble corn farmer
in the high desert of ancient Mexico
and healed the heart
of a ravaged nation
with your compassionate glance.

Please extend your cloak of mercy
to enfold us all,
the weary and disheartened,
the poor and downtrodden,
those who work for peace and justice
    in the world
and the ones who struggle for
    righteousness in our own lives.

Amen.

— Mirabai Starr

Introduction

Woman Clothed with the Sun

She appeared on a remote hilltop in the high desert of Latin America during the height of the Conquest. The indigenous people saw her as a manifestation of Goddess. The Catholic occupiers recognized her as the Virgin Mary. Her compassionate gaze melted the barriers between cultures and faiths, spreading a wave of healing love through a war-ravaged region. She did not come to pay her respects to the privileged and the powerful. She called on the poor and oppressed. She lifted them to their feet, and infused them with dignity and hope.

The Spanish called him Juan Diego; we no longer remember his Nahuatl name. They called *her* Our Lady of Guadalupe. Yet, when the Divine Mother revealed herself to the Aztec peasant we know as Juan Diego, the name she gave herself was in his native tongue. History generally adjusts the reality of the conquered people to match the vision of the conquerors.

The year was 1531. Juan Diego was climbing Tepeyac Hill "on his way to attend to divine things." The European version of this encounter paints a picture of Juan Diego as a humble Indian recently converted to Christianity, who was making a pilgrimage to a chapel in Mexico City (the ancient empire of Tenochtitlan) to hear a sermon. Suddenly, the Virgin Mary appeared to him in what turned out to be the exact location of an indigenous shrine to the Goddess Tonantzin, whose name means "Our Mother."

One of the first known accounts of this miracle is called *Nican Mopohua*. While this historical document clearly conveys the teachings of the Catholic Church, it is written in Nahuatl, the language of the Aztec people of pre-Conquest Mexico. The poetic narrative tells the story of the four apparitions of the Blessed Mother to the peasant Juan Diego.

According to the cherished legend, as he neared the crest of Tepeyac Hill, Juan Diego suddenly heard the most exquisite music flowing down from the summit. It sounded as if every species of bird were singing together in glorious harmony. A sublime radiance appeared in the sky. Juan Diego stood basking in the light and listened until the song ended. He wondered if he was in Xochitalpan, the ancestral place of perfect bliss to which his people believed they were destined to go when they were released at last from their mortal bodies.

Juan Diego was gazing upward toward the source of the celestial music when he heard a woman calling his name from the top of the hill. Suddenly, she materialized in a ball of light. She was the most beautiful girl Juan Diego had ever seen: both vibrant and poised. It looked as if she were "clothed with the sun." He immediately prostrated himself at her feet. She asked him where he was going and he told her he was headed for her "home."

"My dear little son, I love you," she said. "And I want you to know who I am." She then identified herself as "the ever-Virgin Mary, Mother of the True God who gives life and maintains its existence." This God, she reminded the trembling prophet, created all things and lives in all places. "He is the Lord of Heaven and Earth," she said.

Then the Lady told Juan Diego that she had chosen him to be her spokesperson. Like all prophets, he tried to talk her out of it. The Virgin Maria de Guadalupe expressed her desire that a church be built on this holy hill, a sanctuary where anyone who struggles would be able to experience her compassion. "All those who sincerely ask my help in their work and in their sorrows will know my Mother's Heart in this place," she said. When she told him to run to the city and tell the bishop what he had seen and heard, Juan Diego complied, but with serious doubts that this high official would receive him.

He was right. The bishop's servants, suspicious of this illiterate peasant, kept him waiting for hours. When at last Juan Diego was given his minute with the prelate, his worst fears were confirmed: he was brusquely patronized and summarily dismissed. Bishop-elect Fray Juan de Zumarraga condescended to consider the request of the mysterious apparition and told the Indian he could come visit him again sometime. Juan Diego left the bishop's palace feeling completely unworthy of the Mother's mission.

Defeated, Juan Diego returned to the place where she had first appeared to him and found her waiting for him there. As soon as he saw her, Juan's sorrow and doubt melted. The turmoil in his mind was replaced by a preternatural sense of well-being. Still, he implored her to send someone else. Someone more verbal. Someone less Indian. Guadalupe informed him that there were many other people she could have chosen, but that she had elected him. She praised the goodness of his heart and insisted that he was worthy of the task she had set before him. And she sent him back to Bishop Zumarraga.

Once again, Juan waited for hours until the bishop finally called him into his presence. Juan repeated the Mother's request. This time, Zumarraga told him to ask the Lady for a sign as proof of her divine identity. Juan returned to the hill to find Guadalupe waiting for him again. Embarrassed, he relayed the bishop's demand that she prove who she was.

"My little son, am I not your Mother?" she said. "Do not fear. The bishop shall have his sign. Come back to this place tomorrow." And then she blessed him. "Only peace, my little son," Mother Mary said to Juan Diego.

But Juan Diego did not return to the hill the next day. During the night, his uncle, Juan Bernardino, became terminally ill. Juan did not feel he could leave his uncle's side. He remained tending the dying man. As it became clear that Juan Bernardino was not going to recover, Juan Diego finally set out to find a priest to administer the last rites. There was no way to get to the village where the priest lived without passing near Tepeyac

Hill. Ashamed at his inability to comply with the Lady's request, Juan Diego tried to avoid the spot where she had appeared to him in the past. But she materialized in the middle of his detour.

"Do not be distressed, my littlest son. Am I not here with you? Am I not your Mother? Are you not under my shadow of protection?" When Juan offered the excuse of his uncle's impending death, Guadalupe promised him that his uncle was not going to die at this time. "There is no need to engage a priest," she said, "for his health is at this moment restored." Then she ordered Juan Diego to climb to the top of the hill and cut the flowers he would find growing there.

It was December, and very cold. Even in the height of summer, nothing but cactus and thorns had ever grown in the high desert zone of Tepeyac Hill. But Juan Diego did not hesitate. He ran up the slope and discovered hundreds of flowers of every shape and color blooming in wild profusion in the place to which the Lady had guided him. He cut the blossoms and tucked them into his *tilma*, a traditional poncho made of *ayate* cactus fiber. He carried them back to Guadalupe, who arranged them with loving care and then sent Juan Diego back to the bishop.

This time, Zumarraga received him without delay. When Juan Diego opened his cloak to reveal the wildflowers, a cascade of Castilian roses came tumbling out. But it was not the Spanish roses that astounded the bishop and his entourage. Imprinted on the inside of Juan Diego's *tilma* was a perfect image of Mother Mary, exactly as Juan Diego had described her. All doubt vanished and the men fell to their knees in supplication.

The next day, after escorting the bishop to the spot of the apparition, Juan Diego returned home to check on his uncle. Juan Bernardino, as the Lady had promised, was completely cured. Juan Diego's uncle reported that a beautiful woman had appeared to him as he was lying on his deathbed. She was suffused with light. The Lady told Juan Bernardino that she had just sent his nephew to Tenochtitlan with a picture of herself. And then she told him her name: Coatlallope, or, in the local Aztec dialect, "She Who Treads on Snakes."

When the Catholic leaders heard this account, they called her "Nuestra Señora Santa Maria de Guadalupe," importing the name from a much-loved statue of the Virgin Mary found in the village of Guadalupe in Extremadura, Spain, the homeland of many of the conquistadors. The Spanish "Guadalupe," itself a corruption of the original Arabic, meaning "River of Love, River of Light," sounded enough like "Coatlallope" that the Spaniards were able to justify it. The Indians had no choice but to comply.

Bishop Zumarraga had the ancient shrine to Tonantzin destroyed and ordered a church to the Virgin of Guadalupe built on the same site. Juan Diego gave his hut to his uncle and moved into a special room adjacent to Our Lady's chapel, where he spent the rest of his life serving her with singular devotion.

Within six years of the apparition, six million Aztecs converted to Christianity. Where they had persistently resisted the alien male God of the Christian Church, they joyfully embraced a Divine Mother who responded to their despair with comfort and hope, who blessed the emergence of a new people, a people blended of indigenous and European, of earth and sky, a meztizo people, *la raza*.

This Mother continues to shower her blessings on the poor and the grieving throughout this ancient New World of the Americas. She unites the biblical "woman clothed with the sun" and the indigenous serpent goddess. She is Guadalupe-Tonantzin, and she is adored.

The Miraculous Image

The image of Mary emblazoned on Juan Diego's *tilma* has not faded in nearly five hundred years, nor has the fragile *ayate* fabric deteriorated, although it has never been varnished with any protective substance. For the first 116 years, the *tilma* hung in the Basilica of Guadalupe in Mexico City, directly exposed to extreme temperature changes, humidity and flooding, an accidental spill of nitric acid inside the gilded frame, candle and incense smoke, and the kisses and caresses of hundreds of thousands of pilgrims. Now, still residing in the holy basilica, it is shielded by a layer of bulletproof glass and locked in a secret repository every night.

Copies made in 1787 and subjected to similar environmental conditions have all fallen apart, the image faded beyond recognition. The original has been subjected to rigorous chemical analysis but defies consistent identification of the substances that comprise it. In the early 1930s, a team of scientists concluded, simply, "It is a painting . . . without paint!" Even the use of infrared photography cannot conclusively explain an image believers have long since claimed could not possibly have been created by human hands. Microscopic observation reveals no outlines and no brush strokes.

In 1921, a disgruntled factory worker placed a bomb in an offering of flowers at the base of the image of Our Lady of Guadalupe. A cast-iron cross next to the image was completely twisted in the blast. The marble altar rail was shattered. Windowpanes in neighboring houses exploded. But the *tilma* with the image of Our Lady was untouched. Not even a crack appeared in the protective glass around it.

In 1956, a group of ophthalmologists enlarged photographs of Guadalupe's eyes to 2500x magnification. In the center of the iris, they discovered the image of a human being. Closer examination revealed the outline of a native man on his knees, presumed to be Juan Diego, kneeling in adoration of the Divine Mother. Attempts to reproduce similar effects in the eyes of living subjects have failed to produce anything approaching a clear reflection.

The image of Our Lady of Guadalupe is a perfect representation of the mestizo race, a blend of indigenous and European features. She is framed by dozens of broad and narrow rays, which seem to be emanating from her like sunlight. Her skin is dark and her facial structure is finely sculpted. She appears to be walking. The Virgin Mother is pregnant, symbolized by the traditional black maternity band above her waist. Her rose-colored tunic is festooned with flowers and her blue mantle is adorned with stars. Astronomical investigation has revealed that the configuration of the heavenly bodies on her outer garment reflects the position of several easily observable constellations as they would have been seen from Tepeyac Hill on December 12, 1531.

The Virgin Mother rests on a thin crescent moon, symbolizing the cycles of birth, life, death, and rebirth. A dark-skinned angel with a somber countenance and wings of red, green, and white holds her aloft. The small cross around her neck reflects the synthesis of the two cultures. For the indigenous people, the cross represents the four directions, the four seasons, the four phases of human life: childhood, youth, middle age, and old age. For the European Christians, the cross is a sign of Christ's sacrifice for the redemption of humanity.

Mother of the Mestizos

Our Lady of Guadalupe appeared to the Indian Juan Diego only a few short years after Hernán Cortés conquered Mexico for Spain. The conquistadors had initially presented themselves as friends. The Aztecs believed that Cortés was Quetzalcoatl, the divine savior figure who, legend had promised, would return one day when they needed him most, and so they welcomed him and his entourage with joy. Once the Spaniards had insinuated themselves among the indigenous people, however, they proceeded to destroy them. In a concerted act of genocide and enslavement, the conquistadors swiftly eradicated an ancient culture.

The people of Mexico were already suffering from oppression before the Europeans arrived. Aztec religious rituals demanded the blood sacrifice of thousands of citizens a year. The victims were generally drawn from a pool of the poorest and least powerful in society. While it was considered a great honor to be sacrificed to the gods, people lived in a constant state of fear.

Into this bloody mix of violent cultures, Our Lady of Guadalupe extended the hand of mercy, comfort, and protection. She embodied what was most beautiful and loving in each people. She replaced hierarchy with inclusion, patriarchy with tenderness. Our Lady of Guadalupe reconciled the conquest and redeemed the conquered. She drew everyone—European and indigenous— under her blanket of love. And from this place of refuge, the mestizo race was born.

Mexico embraced its hybrid Mother and proceeded to worship her with fierce devotion. This adoration of the Guadalupe spread throughout Latin America, like a drop of dark blue ink in a glass of clear water. Today, she shines from every corner of the Latino world. Our Lady of Guadalupe is earth goddess and she is Virgin Mother of the Son of God. She is the advocate of the native peoples and the living answer to the promise of the Gospel. She is the doorway to Jesus, and the people's affection for her nearly equals their devotion to him.

Images of Our Lady of Guadalupe are found throughout Mexico, Central and South America, and the southwestern United States. She graces storefronts in busy cities, painted into murals in brilliant hues amidst brown-skinned migrant workers pleading for equality. Roadside grottos every few miles hold her image nestled in rock and concrete, a tall glass candle perpetually burning at her feet. She is emblazoned on tee shirts and tattooed onto biceps. She is borrowed to advertise taxi companies and hardware stores, women's circles and bikers' gangs.

She does not discriminate among any of her children. She extends her unconditional love to all who reach for her merciful hand—believers and atheists, Latinos and Anglos, women and men—and they love her back, with equal intensity.

In a world struggling against senseless violence and growing economic disparity, Our Lady of Guadalupe offers a distinctly feminine antidote to the poisons of poverty and war. Where society demands competition, Guadalupe teaches cooperation. In place of consumerism, she models compassionate service. She is not the whitewashed Virgin of the institutionalized Church. She is the radical, powerful, engaged Mother of the People.

Our Lady is not merely a sociopolitical symbol, however. People of all faiths call her Mother. In times of deeply personal grief, they turn to her for comfort. They turn to her for insight. They turn to her for a reminder of what matters most, what endures when all else seems to be lost, what grace may yet be available when we meet fear with love.

Chapter One

She Appears

✦ We Are All Juan Diego ✦

We are all Juan Diego, brought to our knees by suffering, conquered by the conquest. We are simple people, humble craftsmen, single mothers, natives of this land we call Earth. We are doing the best we can. Still, we endure unspeakable hardship. Or we bear silent, helpless witness to the struggles of our people. The people of the Earth.

We look for signs of the divine hand. For the feminine face of the Holy One to appear in the candle flame, or the tortilla, or the crest of a snowcapped mountain. We are looking for mercy.

And yet, when she comes, we do not feel worthy. We have no trouble recognizing her, but we suspect she has made a mistake. Why would you appear to *me? I am nobody. Please, we beg her, go to that man who meditated in a Himalayan cave for thirty years and now gives teachings in cities all over the world. He will know what to do with you. Go to that woman who writes about the death of her child and consoles tens of thousands. She deserves it. I am a factory worker, a soccer mom, a retired cop. Nobody.*

But she will not go away. She gazes upon us with a compassion that melts the most frozen regions of our hearts. You are exactly the one, she says, smiling. Go. Build a temple to me in the midst of your broken life. Invite everyone in. Tell them they are forgiven. Assure them they have done nothing wrong in the first place. Remind them that I told them I was coming long ago, in a recurring dream they had as children, during the winter their first love left them, that day they discovered they were going to have a baby. Let them know I am here.

And that I am the True Friend who will never leave them.

We are all Juan Diego. The Mother appears when we need her most. And when she comes, she so thoroughly dazzles us with her radiant beauty that all the resistance of our minds drops away like ripe fruit, and we raise our faces in adoration. Her love heals the burnt garden of our hearts and now, again, everything bursts into bloom. A miracle of blossoms.

God of power and mercy,
you blessed the Americas at Tepeyac
with the presence of the Virgin Mary
    of Guadalupe.

May her prayers help all men and women
to accept each other as brothers and sisters.

Through your justice present in our hearts,
may your peace reign in the world.

— Mirabai Starr,
slightly adapted from a prayer of the Catholic Church

She Appears

Hail, O Empress of America

Hail, O Empress of America,
our dear Queen without a stain.
Guadalupe is your title
And the throne from which you reign
Is Mount Tepeyac made blessed
When you came to earth again.

Mother Mary graced our country
With her loving presence rare.
She appeared to Juan Diego
Sending him with gentle care
To the bishop with a message
That she wished a shrine built there.

"Build a temple to my honor,
Where my mother heart may reign,
Calling all with sweet compassion;
None will come to me in vain.
All in labor or affliction
Strength and peace will find again."

The good bishop, wisely prudent,
Begged a sign of Heaven's Queen;
And the gracious Lady answered
In a manner sweet, serene;
Working miracles, inspiring
Hope through ages yet unseen.

She commanded Juan Diego
Gather roses fair and bright
Which she caused to bloom in winter
On a barren, rocky height,
On the twelfth day of December—
Blessed day! O blessed site!

She arranged them in Juan's mantle
Saying with a smile benign:
"Take these to the holy bishop,
Here he has the heavenly sign.
Do not look within your mantle
Till the bishop you will find."

When Juan opened his poor mantle
To the bishop's great surprise,
Roses fell in shower of glory

Spreading their sweet perfume wide.
But the prelate knelt in reverence;
Greater marvel met his eyes.

There upon the cheap, rough tilma,
Painted by an art divine,
Was the portrait of Our Lady,
Queen and Mother for all time,
Come to dwell in our dear country
Blessing souls with gifts sublime.

Hail, O Empress of America,
Guadalupe is your name.
Please accept our humble homage,
Bless our hearts and homes again.
Keep us loyal to our Savior
Till with Him and you we reign.

— Sister Regina, the Missionary Catechist

He was looking over there, toward the top of
 the hill where the sun rises,
from where the splendid celestial
 song emanated.

And when the singing suddenly ceased,
when it was no longer heard,
he heard someone calling to him from the
 top of the hill.

They called: "Juanito, Juan Dieguito."

He then dared to go where they called him;
his heart felt no agitation nor did anything
 trouble him;
on the contrary, he felt extremely happy
 and content.

He climbed up the hill to see where they
 called him from.
And when he reached the top of the hill,
A maiden standing there saw him.

She called for him to come closer . . .

— Nican Mopohua

When he stood before Her,
he was filled with admiration
for the way Her perfect grandeur
exceeded all imagination:

Her dress shone like the sun;
it seemed to shimmer,
and the rock,
the crag on which She stood,
seemed to throw rays of light.

Her radiance
was like that of precious stones,
like bracelets
(everything most beautiful) they seemed.
The earth appeared to glow
with the brilliance
of a rainbow in the mist.

And the mesquite and the prickly pears
and the rest of the shrubs
that ordinarily grow there

looked like emeralds.
Their leaves looked like turquoise.
and their trunks,
their thorns,
their thistles,
glimmered like gold.

— Nican Mopohua

A great sign appeared in the sky,
A woman clothed with the Sun,
with the moon under her feet,
and on her head a crown of twelve stars.

She was with child,
and wailed aloud in pain
as she labored to give birth.

Then another sign appeared in the sky;
it was a huge red dragon,
with seven heads and ten horns,
and on its heads were seven diadems.
Its tail swept away a third of the stars in the sky

She Appears

and hurled them down to the earth.
Then the dragon stood before the woman
    about to give birth,
to devour her child when she gave birth.
She gave birth to a son, a male child,
destined to rule all the nations with an iron rod.
Her child was caught up to God and his throne.

The woman herself fled into the desert
where she had a place prepared by God,
that there she might be taken care of . . .

When the dragon saw
that it had been thrown down to the earth,
it pursued the woman
who had given birth to the male child.

But the woman was given
the two wings of the great eagle,
so that she could fly to her place in the desert,
where, far from the serpent,
she was taken care of . . .

— Revelation 12

As he neared the hill called Tepeyac,
dawn was breaking.
He heard singing from the top of the hill,
like the song of many fine birds.
When their song ended,
the hill seemed to answer them,
exceedingly soft, delightful.
Its song surpassed the songs
of the coyoltotl and the tzinitzcan
and of the other fine birds.

Juan Diego halted,
and asked himself:
"Perhaps I am only dreaming?
Perhaps I am only half-awake.
Where am I?
Where do I find myself?
Could I be in the place the ancestors spoke of,
our forefathers and our grandfathers:
in the land of flowers,
in the land of maize,
of our flesh, of our sustenance;
in the celestial land?"

— Nican Mopohua

Juan Diego:
Ever since I saw Nonache,
I have lost myself in her.
Oh Nonache, dearest Lady,
To be with you I'd prefer.

And to gaze upon you, Mother,
Oh Most Sovereign Epitath,
Please don't think that I'm ungrateful
If I take another path.

For it's not because I'm hiding,
That's not what it's all about.
It's because I am most shameful
That the bishop harbors doubt.

He believes not what I tell him,
But I make a solemn vow:
Though you're far from my poor vision,
In my heart you're with me now.

Guadalupe:
Do not think to hide thus from me,
For I dwell in every place.

Juan Diego:

Dearest Mother, of your message
Every thought I do embrace.
Your own words the great archbishop
Would believe if from above.

This I say to you, my Lady,
But it's not for lack of love.
I would serve your radiant beauty,
Since I am your very slave.
But I hang my head in silence,
And remain thus, to my grave.

Guadalupe:

Although Juan, you make excuses,
My ambassador you'll be.
For I find none other worthy.
You were chosen here by me.

—Larry Torres,
in *The Four Apparitions of Guadalupe*

"I beg of you, my Lady, my Queen, my little Girl, to send one of the nobles, who is well-liked, who is well-known, respected, revered, honored, to carry your kind breath, your kind word, so that he will be believed.

"Because I am really only a man of the land, a *mecapal,* a hand-cart, a lowly man, a wing. I myself must be led, carried. That place where you send me is no place for me, my little Virgin, my youngest Daughter, my Lady, my Girl. Please, forgive me: I will alter your countenance, your heart with grief; I will make you angry; I will cause you displeasure, my Lady, my Mistress."

The perfect Virgin, deserving of honor and reverence, answered him: "Listen, the youngest of my sons, be assured that I do not lack servants, messengers, whom I can command to carry my breath, my word, to carry out my will. But it is quite necessary that you, personally, go, plead, that by your intercession my desire, my will, be carried out . . ."

Juan Diego, for his part, answered Her . . . "My Lady, my Queen, my Little Girl, let me not alter your face, your heart, with grief. I will go gladly to carry out your word, your breath. Nothing will stop me. I cherish the path all the more for its obstacles. I will go carry out your word, but I may not be heard, and if I am heard, I may not be believed . . .

"For now, I respectfully bid you farewell, my youngest Daughter, little Maiden, my Lady, my Girl. Rest a while longer . . ."

— Nican Mopohua

It is you I seek, Juan Diego.
Please approach, beloved son.
Though you stumble toward the city,
Your true journey's just begun.

You must seek the old archbishop
In his palace rich and clean,
To report this apparition
And the signs that you have seen.

She Appears

You must speak of my volition
That a temple be erect
In this kingdom that I'll visit,
This dear Mexico elect.

I will be a source of refuge
To all dwellers here who seek
My divinest intercession.
Do not doubt that which I speak.

For behold, I'm with you always,
At your side, so pure and meek.

— Larry Torres,
in *The Four Apparitions of Guadalupe*

And the Celestial Queen then ordered him to climb to the top of the hill, where he had seen her before.

She told him: "Go up there, my son, the youngest, to the top of the hill, where you saw me and I gave you orders. There you will see a variety of flowers. Cut them, gather them, put them all together. Then come back down here, bring them here, to me."

Juan Diego then went up the hill, and when he reached the summit he was astonished by all the blooming flowers, the open blossoms, so lovely and beautiful, when it was still not their season, because this was really the season of the harshest frost.

They released a soft fragrance, like precious pearls, as if filled with nocturnal dew. He then began to cut them, he gathered them all, and put them in the hollow of his cloak.

Certainly the summit of the hill was not a place where flowers grew. There was only an abundance of crags, thistles, thorns, prickly pear, mesquite, and perhaps an occasional wildflower sprouted. It was then the month of December, when the ice devours, destroys everything.

Then he immediately came back down, he came to bring the Celestial Girl the different flowers that he had gone to cut. And when She saw him, She picked them up in Her venerable hands. Then she placed them back in the hollow of his *ayate*.

— Nican Mopohua

Juan Diego addresses the Archbishop:

I am just a lowly Indian.
By Juan Diego I am known.
When I left my home this morning
Through the hillsides all alone
I did meet a sovereign lady
With a crown that brightly shone.

Her pink robe was all bespangled,
And with brilliant stars besown.
And the mantle that surrounds her
Looks just like the evening skies.
For the moon is at her footsteps
And the sun behind her shines.

It was hard to gaze upon her
And the angel who attends
Looking up at her and listening
To the message that she sends.

For the lady sent these portents
Which I bring before your sight
So that you may build a temple
On that lonesome little site.

— Larry Torres,
in *The Four Apparitions of Guadalupe*

BUSINESS REPLY MAIL

FIRST-CLASS MAIL   PERMIT NO. 493   BOULDER, CO.

POSTAGE WILL BE PAID BY ADDRESSEE:

SOUNDS TRUE
CATALOG
PO BOX 8010
BOULDER CO 80306-9886

NO POSTAGE
NECESSARY
IF MAILED
IN THE
UNITED STATES

Rare, useful learning programs with you in mind

THE SOUNDS TRUE CATALOG

...is your direct source for inspirational and informative audio and video recordings about meditation, psychology, spirituality and religion, health and healing, relationships, personal discovery, creativity, sacred music, and much more. Call toll free 800-333-9185, visit www.soundstrue.com, or mail this card to Sounds True.

Yes, please send me a free catalog:

PRINT NAME

ADDRESS

CITY　　　　　　　　　　STATE　　ZIP

EMAIL ADDRESS (Learn about new releases and special offers.
Note: We never share email addresses with other companies.)

May we send a free catalog to one of your friends?

PRINT FRIEND'S NAME

ADDRESS

CITY　　　　　　　　　　STATE　　ZIP

STBN4

Holy Flower of God

With delight I have seen
the opening of perfumed flowers
in thy presence, Holy Mary.

Beside the still waters,
I have heard Holy Mary singing:

I am the precious plant with hidden buds;
I was created by the One and Perfect God;
I am supreme among His creatures.

. . . In the beauty of the flowers
did God create you, Holy Mary!
And re-created you,
through a sacred painting.

Delicately was your image painted
and on the sacred canvas
your soul was concealed.
All is perfect and complete in its presence,
and there, God willing,
I shall dwell forever.

Who will follow my example?
Who will hasten to come after me?

Oh, let us kneel around her!
Let us sing sweet songs
and scatter flowers in her presence!

Weeping, I commune with my own soul,
that the whole purpose of my song
may be made known,
and that the desire of my heart
may be fulfilled
in the building of the Virgin's house.
Then shall my soul be at rest there.

And it shall know perfume
greater than the fragrance of flowers,
And my hymn will rise in praise
of the beautiful bloom
which forms her perpetual adornment!

The flower of the cocoa
spreads its fragrance.
The flower of the pomoya
perfume every road
leading to this holy place.
And there I, the sweet singer, will dwell.
Hark, O hearken to my hymn of joy!

—"Teponazcuicatl,"
an ancient Mexican song adapted to Christianity

Moon of the Mexican Sea, a new sky.
The son of God wished to stay here,
and here the Mother of God's son,
in her lasting miracle,
wished to perpetuate herself . . .

Precious Pearl,
Imperial Eagle,
Moon without descent . . .

The Queen threw the entire sun on her back,
and with no assistance, with no support,
persevering through the centuries,
today like the first day she remains,
    and endures.

And the two Temples? They aged.
And their cedars? Moths ate them.
And the stones? They turned to dust:
And the image? It competes with the eternal
and surpasses the world with persistency,
Heaven with durations.

She Appears

Much does the temple resemble the world,
this Marian temple of Guadalupe,
founded in the unpredictable location of the
    Mexican Lake,
but with the stability of that beautiful Sky,
transcribed by his Master on the *Ayate;*
and if the temple were to copy his image,
in this temple would be an image of the Sky.

— Juan de Goicochea

Heavenly Protectress

The Miracle composed of flowers real,
American Protectress heavenly,
Who Rose of Mexico now comes to be
Appearing as a Rose of old Castille;

She who, not dragon—whose rebellious zeal
She tamed in Patmos—marks pridefully
Pure seat of her own pure sublimity,
Intelligence thus far as great ideal;

Now Heaven, that copies her, mysterious
Her signs celestial a second time
Sums up in figures clear of flowers then:

No less thus give her copy beauteous
The Flowers of your verses quite sublime,
The marvel of your learned artistic pen.

— Sor Juana Ines de la Cruz

She Appears

Only with You

If the moon at your feet yields space
and forges the pedestal of your beauty,
if breaking through the clouds as if by surprise,
the sun shines with the rays of your life,

if you have come, Maiden, your head
covered with a mantle of stars,
if the radiance of your eyes only expresses
that the light of love is already kindled,

if you are, Virgin, the flame that God the Father
left to light our way,
if you are "the river of light," my sweet Mother,

that only clarity has sown,
I come so that you might illumine my destiny,
because there is nothing like you
    anywhere else.

— Monsignor P. Guizar V.

Mary, Virgin of Guadalupe

Dark lady, you smile at me across
    the mountains
the secret smile of ancient people.
What thoughts do you send me,
    dark beautiful lady?

Will you someday tell me when I come
    with great
armfuls of roses
over the mysterious mountains to
    your feet?

Dear, dark queen, will you give me too
lovely roses in December?

— Anne B. Quinn

Build Me a Temple

God the Mother makes impossible demands on us all. "Build me a temple," she says. As if we could simply drop our rakes and hoes in the middle of planting season and rush off to the Vatican for papal permission. We wouldn't make it past the gates of the city. Who could afford the plane ticket?

Maybe we are reading too much into these divine orders. Maybe the Mother is simply reminding us that the first and most important thing is to make a shrine in our hearts and bow down to her there. A place where we leave our tools and our lists, our checkbooks and our uniforms, at the door. Where we enter and kneel and lay our troubles at her most merciful feet.

"Convince the bishop that I have come and I am real and that he needs to fully cooperate with this temple-building task." As if that were so easy. As if we could just stride up to the authority figures of this

world and insist that they drop everything and listen to us, whom nobody has ever heard of, because we had a vision. They would lock us up.

Try this: "Dear Mr. President, I have gathered the names of a few hundred of my closest friends (known as We The People) to suggest that you consider diverting those bomb funds to feed hungry children. We understand that you feel the citizens of our great land are under threat, but we submit to you that all people are one, and that you must lend the full energy of your power to swiftly alleviate the suffering of the oppressed members of the Human Family. With love from, Nobody Special." Who knows? The Commander in Chief's heart could fly open as he dedicates himself to the divine feminine in everyone, everywhere, forever more.

The Mother says, "Go up to that barren plateau in deep winter and gather the profusion of flowers you will find there. Show them to the world as a sign from Me." Flowers in December? In the desert?

Just go. Climb the mountain trails you already know and love. Find the flowers blooming in the snow. Unravel the paradox. Desert and garden are interchangeable terms for our own souls: sometimes barren and wild and then, at the most unexpected moments, abundant and harmonious. There are two miracles unfolding here. Yes, the Divine Mother has brought forth roses in winter; and also, the hard spiritual work you have done on yourself has yielded harvest at last.

Chapter Two

Blossoms of Mercy

◈ Say Yes to Everything ◈

Mother of Mercy, I cannot hold my life another minute. Take it from me. I offer you the gift of my brokenness. It is all I have left to give. Nothing has worked out the way I dreamed it as a child, as a young lover, as a student and a rebel and an idealistic worshipper of God. And the things I would have feared most have come true. I do not know how to put one breath in front of the other. Nothing makes any sense anymore. I place my weary head in your lap, Mother. I surrender.

And I, Mother, come to you whole. While people in my own community have been ravaged by tragedy, my life has been free from great sorrow. While children all over the world go to sleep hungry, I have the luxury of trying to lose weight. A fight with my lover feels like the end of the world, until I remember that bombs are exploding in busy marketplaces in ancient cities far away and entire families are destroyed. Take the comfort and prosperity in my life, Mother, and distribute it. Teach me to take responsibility for the privilege into which I have been born.

Mother of Mercy, your hand is not the hand of wrath and castigation. Yours is not the gift of fiery redemption. Your blessing comes as gentle breath, as tender forgiveness, as a smile of unconditional love. You know our pain, Mother, because you, too, have suffered unspeakable anguish. Your compassion rains upon us not from some lofty sweetness, but rises from the depths of your own encounter with blood and tears, with betrayal and acceptance.

As you said yes to everything, Mother, to God the Father and God the Son and God the Spirit of Holiness, to brutal persecution and impossible grief, to invisible angels and visible prophets, to your own unshakable strength and power, teach me to say yes to my life, yes to the call to be of service in this broken world.

Here I will hear
their weeping and their sorrows . . .
their necessities and misfortunes . . .

Listen, and let it penetrate your heart . . .

Do not be troubled and
weighed down with grief.
Do not fear any illness or vexation,
anxiety or pain.

Am I not here who am your Mother?
Are you not under my shadow
    and protection?
Am I not your fountain of life?
Are you not in the folds of my mantle?
In the crossing of my arms?

Is there anything else you need?

> — The Blessed Virgin to Juan Diego,
> December 12, 1531, in *The Wonder
> of Guadalupe*, Francis Johnston

Our Lady of Guadalupe

Into the nightmare
of a people still haunted
by their ancestral past,
just outside Mexico City,
on a hill
in a little spot
known simply as Tepeyac,
came a mere
slip of a girl
draped in a starlit
turquoise mantle,
haloed by a mandorla,
of tongues of fire
and perched on that
moon of dark memory.

Mary,
ever so slightly
nodding,
with the most tender
gentle
humble

and loving gaze
one could ever imagine.

She appeared pregnant,
full of the Word,
burning with the
Love within.

She brought roses
to the skeptical,
wonders and a teaching
to the very Church
she images
and left,
her blessed visit
ever-sealed
on the clothes
of a poor man.

Her message
rings out anew
in this year of
Jubilee,
this Favorable Time:

> "I listen to your
> weeping and solace
> all your sorrows
> and your sufferings."
>
> — Father William Hart McNichols,
> in *Fire Above, Water Below*

Blessed Virgin Mary of Guadalupe,
Mother of our Lord,

I call upon you this day
to be my special friend here on earth,
today and all the days of my life.

I ask you to be my special protectress
and I place all my thoughts, words and deeds
at your feet.

I ask you to be my guide
and guardian.

May I please the Holy One
in all I do and say.

— "Autom," a pamphlet of the Catholic Church

"Am I not here who am thy Mother—
What dost thou fear?"

Deep in the tangled brushwood of my hours,
You are a sudden clearing, *Madre mia,*
Amid the choke of thorn,
Incredible rose.

And where my fears sit huddled in their trembling,
You are a soft word spoken, O Maria,
In heart's cacophony, a splendid chord!

Brave alabaster out of hope-shards built,
What need I dream of beauty, I who know
Curve of your cheek, the raven hair low-winging,
Soft swell of lip, the delicate flight of brow!

Exuberance, be hedged in Christ oh! Sweetly
By this rumorous smile's so wistful bands;
And sorrow, find your meaning, find your haven
    In this gentle fold of olive hands.

Authentic glimpse of heaven, *Madre mia,*
Your image my supernal dividend
On sorrow, and my pledge past all devising.

Virgin of Guadalupe

Of paradisal day. What shall I fear
Of pain, of death, of diverse ignominy
When you are here, Maria, when you are here.

— Mother Mary Francis, P.C.C.

∽ To Our Lady Dark Yet Fair ∽

O hail, thou Virgen de Guadalupe!
Unfailing refuge, our solace in days of grief,
Radiant Queen so kind, our Mother of
    sweet relief
¡Viva la Virgen de Guadalupe!

Lovely Maid, fairest star above the sea!
Advocate e'er gracious of clemency and love,
Deign to listen to our pleas, O mother above
¡Viva la Virgen de Guadalupe!

Yea, O Lady of Guadalupe; O meek and
gentlest One, take heed to our groaning;
For oft we stumble and raise to thee our moaning
¡Viva la Virgen de Guadalupe!

Golden gate of heav'n, thou radiant portal;
Unstained by sin, blissful queen of heav'n
and earth, Aid me that I may love Him
whom you did give birth
¡Viva la Virgen de Guadalupe!

Daughter of God, thou queen of royalty,
Ave Maria! With joyful hearts we hail thee!
Look on us so kindly, O Blessed Virgin Mary!
¡Viva la Virgen de Guadalupe!

Unfailing refuge and sweetest Mother; Pearl of
grace so fair, fail not thine children to care, E'er
our sweetest Advocate who did God once bear
¡Viva la Virgen de Guadalupe!

— Jeong-Bo Shim

Please remember,
O most gracious Virgin Mary of Guadalupe,
that in your celestial apparitions on the mount of Tepeyac,
you promised to show your compassion and pity towards all who,
loving and trusting you,
seek your help and call upon you
in their necessities and afflictions.

You promised to hearken to our supplications,
to dry our tears and to give us consolation and relief.

Never was it known that anyone who fled to your protection,
implored your help, or sought your intercession,
either for the common welfare, or in personal anxieties,
was left unaided.

Inspired with this confidence, we fly to you,
O Mary, ever-Virgin Mother of the True Divine!

Though grieving under the weight of our imperfections,

we come to prostrate ourselves in your
    majestic presence,
certain that you will fulfill your
    merciful promises.

We are full of hope that,
standing beneath your shadow
    and protection,
nothing will trouble or afflict us,
nor need we fear illness, or misfortune, or any
    other sorrow.

You have decided to remain with us
through your glorious image,
you who are our Mother, our health, and
    our life.

Placing ourselves beneath your maternal gaze
and having access to you in all our necessities,
we need do nothing more.

O Holy Mother of God,
Do not reject our petitions,
but in your mercy hear and answer us.

— Mirabai Starr,
slightly adapted from a prayer of the Catholic Church

Novena in Honor of Our Lady of Guadalupe

First Day:
Dearest Lady of Guadalupe, fruitful Mother of holiness, teach me your ways of gentleness and strength. Hear my humble prayer offered with heartfelt confidence to beg this favor.

Second Day:
O Mary, conceived without stain, I come to your throne of grace to share the fervent devotion of your faithful Mexican children who call to you under the glorious Aztec title of Guadalupe. Obtain for me a lively faith to recognize and carry out the divine will always.

Third Day:
O Mary, whose Immaculate Heart was pierced by seven swords of grief, help me to walk valiantly amid the sharp thorns strewn across my pathway. Obtain for me the strength to be a true imitator of you. This I ask you, my dear Mother.

Fourth Day:
Dearest Mother of Guadalupe, I beg you for a fortified will to imitate your divine Son's charity, to always seek the good of others in need.

Fifth Day:
O most holy Mother, I beg you to obtain for me pardon of all my errors, abundant graces to serve the Holy One more faithfully from now on, and lastly, the grace to praise Him with you forever.

Sixth Day:
Mary, Mother of vocations, multiply contemplative inclinations and fill the earth with sanctuaries and retreats that will be light and warmth for the world, safety in stormy nights. Beg the Holy One to send us many spiritual guides.

Seventh Day:
O Lady of Guadalupe, we beg you that parents live a holy life and educate their children in a sacred manner; that children honor and follow the directions of their parents; that all members of the family pray and worship together.

Eighth Day:
With my heart full of the most sincere veneration, I prostrate myself before you, O Mother, to ask you to obtain for me the grace to fulfill the duties of my state in life with faithfulness and constancy.

Ninth Day:
O God, You have been pleased to bestow upon us unceasing favors by having placed us under the special protection of the Most Blessed Virgin Mary. Grant us, your humble servants, who rejoice in honoring her today upon earth, the happiness of seeing her face to face in heaven.

Hail Mary, full of grace. The Lord is with thee. Blessed art thou amongst women, and blessed is the fruit of thy womb, Jesus. Holy Mary, Mother of God, pray for us sinners, now and at the hour of our death. Amen.

— Mirabai Starr,
slightly adapted from a novena of the Catholic Church

Know and be assured . . .
that I am the Perfect Forever
    Virgin Holy Mary,
Mother of the true God for Whom
    we live,
Creator of people,
Lord of the nearness and
    the immediacy,
Lord of Heaven, Lord of the earth.

I greatly desire, I greatly wish
for my sacred home to be
    erected here,
where I can show Him,
exalt Him by manifesting Him:
I will give Him to the people
with all my personal love,
with my compassionate gaze,
with my help, my salvation.

Because I am truly your
   compassionate mother,
yours and of all men who
   are united
   on this land.
And of all the other different races
   of men;
those who love me,
those who cry out for me,
those who seek me,
those who trust me;
because there I will listen to
   their weeping,
   their woes,
to remedy, to cure all their
   different troubles,
their misery, their suffering.

— Nican Mopohua

Ave María

Oh Virgin of the Dawn, Ave María
the Father of the harvest is with you
to cause the flour of His Wheat
to be converted into the Bread of your joy.

Blessed for being a woman, Ave María,
because your virginal womb gave shelter
to the Eternal Word, redeeming friend,
Who, with His Flesh, ransomed mine.

Lady of the Evening, Ave María,
pray for us, sinners,
now and in the hour of that day

On which the Dead will command us, "Come,"
and make our interior responses
gladden the Angels.
Amen.

— Monsignor J. Guizar V.

Our Lady of Guadalupe, Mystical Rose,
carry our petitions to the House of God.

Protect our spiritual guides,
help all those who invoke you in
    their necessities,
and since you are the ever Virgin Mary,
and Mother of the True Divine,
obtain for us from your most holy Son
the grace of keeping our faith,
of sweet hope in the midst of the
    bitterness of life,
of burning charity,
and the precious gift of
    final perseverance.

Amen.

— Mirabai Starr, slightly adapted from
a prayer of the Catholic Church

The Favor of Guadalupe

The air sings if your voice kisses it,
the water dances if your light focuses upon it,
the earth is heaven if your foot touches it,
the fire is glory if it expresses your love.

And if my soul enters into your gaze,
repentant of its mad life,
you return it purified, and from your
    lovely mouth
a word begins to blossom:

You call me "son" with tender accent
as you said to Juan Diego the day
on which the winter was clothed with roses.

You draw, then, my steps towards yourself
and you offer me your fountain of joy,
placing me in the crossing of your arm.

— Monsignor J. Guizar V.

Immaculate Heart of Mary,
Heart of my Mother,
Our Lady of Guadalupe,
I unite to your purity,
your sanctity,
your zeal,
and your love,
all my thoughts, words, acts,
and sufferings this day,
that there may be nothing in me
that does not become through You,
a pleasure to Christ,
a gain to souls,
and an act of reparation
for the offenses against your Heart.

— From "Morning Offering,"
a prayer of the Catholic Church

Madre mia de Guadalupe por tus cuatro apariciones, Antes de cuatro dias, remedia mis aflicciones.
Madre mia de Guadalupe por tus cuatro apariciones, Antes de cuatro dias, remedia mis aflicciones.
Madre mia de Guadalupe por tus cuatro apariciones, Antes de cuatro dias, remedia mis aflicciones.
Madre mia de Guadalupe por tus cuatro apariciones, Antes de cuatro dias, remedia mis aflicciones.

Sweet Mother of Guadalupe, through your four apparitions, Within four days, please heal my afflictions.

Sweet Mother of Guadalupe, through your four apparitions, Within four days, please heal my afflictions.

Sweet Mother of Guadalupe, through your four apparitions, Within four days, please heal my afflictions.

Sweet Mother of Guadalupe, through your
  four apparitions, Within four days, please
  heal my afflictions.

— Old New Mexico healing prayer

⁌ Face to Face ⁌

Let me in stillness contemplate your eyes
and through these eyes know your soul.
I want to drink of the glorious spring
that sustains you in plenitude of grace.

To pass through your black pupils
to the brightness of your heaven of cobalt,
where the stars, which bring light
to your precious mantle, are palpitating.

To enter your garden of Indian soil,
to see how your celestial roses
mold with exquisite beauty your living image
and continue flowering in your gown.

I long to follow the path of your maternal love
in the iris of your living eyes,
to fill to the brim my happiness because I am
    your child
and to see your light, as Juan Diego saw it . . .

— Monsignor J. Guizar V.

Definition

You are all light. Even your shadow
clarifies, gladdens, soothes, perfumes, illumines
and undoes the sheaves of penumbra
because of which the sun, in all its
    splendors, dims.

You are all of God. Although you are ours,
since you carry in your voice a Mexican timbre.
There is nothing in you that is not of God,
    the Father,
and in you He manifests grace in all
    its fullness.

You are all sweetness. If the veins
of us, your children, carry offenses,

with only the smile of your lips
you give us balm to heal our wounds.

You are all peace. The heavens proclaim
that the love of your being always appears
with memories of the olive branch and the dove
in the flag of your dark skin.

You are all garden. Noble attribute,
for having made of your womb the delicate clay
where the Living Seed grew,
and to God and to us, you delivered the Fruit.

You are all song. And so much so
that by you the *cenzontle* is provided with
    its voice
to give glory, when it joyously sings,
to the Father, to the Son, and to the Holy Spirit.

You are all woman. Sublime Virgin,
maternal tenderness, pure caress,
altar of grace where God officiates
the mystery of love which redeems us.

— Monsignor J. Guizar V.

O Immaculate Virgin,
Mother of the true God
and Mother of God's House,
who from this place
reveal your clemency and your pity
to all those who ask for your protection,
hear the prayer that we address to you with
    filial trust,
and present it to your Son, our Inspiration.

Mother of Mercy,
Teacher of hidden and silent sacrifice,
to you, who come to meet us,
we dedicate on this day
all our being and all our love.
We also dedicate to you our life, our work,
our joys, our infirmities, and our sorrows.

Grant peace, justice, and prosperity to
    our peoples;
for we entrust to your care
all that we have and all that we are,
our Lady and Mother.

Our Lady of Guadalupe

We wish to be entirely yours
and to walk with you along the way of
> complete faithfulness;
hold us always with your loving hand.

Virgin of Guadalupe,
Mother of the Americas,
we pray to you for all spiritual guides,
that they may lead the faithful
> along paths of intense aliveness,
of love and humble service of the Holy One
> and souls.

Contemplate this immense harvest,
and intercede with the Lord
that He may instill a hunger for holiness
in the whole people of God,
and grant abundant vocations to mystics and
> spiritual teachers,
strong in the faith and passionate dispensers
> of God's mysteries.

Grant to our homes the grace of loving and
> respecting life,
with the same love with which you nurtured
> the Word of God.

Blossoms of Mercy

Blessed Virgin Mary,
protect our families,
so that they may always be united,
and bless the upbringing of our children.

Our hope,
look upon us with compassion,
teach us to go continually to God and,
if we fall, help us to rise again,
to return to Him,
who gives peace to the soul . . .

Thus, Most Holy Mother,
with the peace of God in our conscience,
with our hearts free from evil and hatred,
we will be able to bring to all
true joy and true peace.

Amen.

— Adapted by Mirabai Starr

Guadalupe to Juan Diego:
Never doubt what I am saying,
For my son, on this small plot
With one whim, the world was created.
Now I leave for you this sign,
So that all may come to marvel
At this sacramental shrine.

Where I'm treading now and always
Will the waters from above
Spring and never cease their flowing
Like my ever-burning love.

— Larry Torres,
in *The Four Apparitions of Guadalupe*

Wise as Serpents, Harmless as Doves

Mother of Mercy, you teach us that we do not have to be healed to be healers. That by stretching our hearts to forgive others, we grow in capacity to forgive ourselves. That battered by our own difficult circumstances, we can nevertheless reach out to those who are suffering and offer genuine solace.

Dear Mother, do not let us be selfish with our love. Let us spread it indiscriminately, in spite of all advice to the contrary. Let us soften our hearts and yield when everything in us wants to strap on thick armor and strike back: yield to the raging driver who ran over our best friend on a quiet street in early spring; yield to the man who authorizes secret torture; yield to the troubled birth of a child destined to die before she ever learns to recognize her father's face; yield to the tsunami and the forest fire, to cancer and drug addiction.

And yet, Divine Mother, do not let us practice idiot compassion. Let us be wise as serpents and harmless as doves. Let us open our eyes at the same time that we are opening our hearts. Give us the courage to stand up against senseless cruelty and, replete with lovingkindness and empty of rancor, say no when no is what's required: no, you may not commit atrocities in our name; or speak to or about your mother with disrespect; or steal resources from the poor to line your overflowing coffers; or force your mindless infrastructure on what little remains of our pristine wilderness.

Guadalupe, you who give voice to the voiceless and stand up for the disenfranchised, help us to put aside our own problems long enough to see that far too many members of the Human Family are dropping under the burden they carry. That our brother animals and sister trees are in danger of extinction. That the earth herself is crying in anguish while we obsess about not being rich or famous or beautiful enough. Let us breathe deeply and admit: we are far from whole, but we are available to bring about wholeness wherever we can.

It is in this unconditional willingness to show up and bear witness to others, Beloved Mother, that we may find, again and again, freedom from our own suffering.

Chapter Three

Mother of the People

~ Rebel Mother ~

Rebel Mother, embolden us now. Fill our depleted hearts with the courage to speak for those who cannot speak for themselves. Let us not turn away from the needs of our brothers and sisters. Help us to graciously accept the consequences of speaking truth to power.

Once upon a time, the Church forgot who they were. They forgot who you were, Blessed Mother, and forgot your Holy Son. In Europe, they trampled their closest cousins, the Jews and the Muslims. And then they moved onto a continent that had been inhabited for millennia, called it a New World, and violated the sacred cultures they found there.

That's when you rose from the earth with a great battle cry of love, Madre Mia. You tore through the illusion of separation and demanded unity. Your face was the familiar face of the earth, warm and brown. Your language was the native tongue of the conquered people. You redeemed the people's blood with your tears of compassion, Mother. With hands outstretched, rather than sword uplifted, you reclaimed their connection to their ancestral land. They recognized their true selves in you.

We need to remember to call on you, Mother of All Peoples, in this work for justice. We cannot effect change by ourselves. We must resist the impulse to act from anger, Mother, and remember to draw from your fathomless well of mercy. We have to cultivate stillness and self-awareness, Guadalupe, before we forget that we are all One: the oppressors and the oppressed, the greedy and the hungry, the violent and the guardians of peace.

Then, with you at our side, Divine Revolutionary, we can charge into the unknown and break the chains of your captive people.

> God,
> in Your concern
> and love
> for Your people
> You gave a priceless gift
> to the Americas:
> the appearance of Mary,
> Mother of Jesus,
> at Guadalupe.
>
> Help the countries
> of this continent
> to live with one another
> in peace,
> unity,
> and brotherhood.
>
> Amen.
>
> — Prayer of the Catholic Church

Known as Tonantzin among the Nahuatls, but also as Saint Moon, Queen of Nature, or Earth Mother in other parts of the Americas, *la Guadalupana* is the poor people's agent, not bound by form, or by a name, or by the limitations of time, space, or race.

She returns as the vessel of the indigenous spirit, as the shamed land crying back its blood. She returns speaking the inflections of an ancient tongue, before Christianity, beyond Christianity.

La Diosa's face is resurrected in all the faces of all the mothers, of all the young women and children of our *gente*. She is among the bearers of the myths, the rites, and the ancient quests.

She reemerges throughout the hemisphere with many titles—*Nuestra Señora de San Juan de los Lagos, Nuestra Señora de Quiche, Nuestra Señora de Altagracia, Nuestra Señora de Caridad del Cobre, Nuestra*

Señora de Providencia, Nuestra Señora de Monserrate—and she often appears dark, like the poor who honor her, who embody her with their resistance, with their collective memory and identity.

I see her and I see them all, tribes of this continent, tribes of other continents, who are daily born of woman, Mother Creator. I see them and I know that Tonantzin has risen again and again.

— Luis J. Rodriguez,
in *Forgive Me, Mother, for My Crazy Life*

Our Lady of Guadalupe is a warrior.

From the beginning, since the sixteenth century when the indigenous people of Mexico needed the sensibility and generosity of a deity who understood their horrendous suffering, she has never abandoned that role.

And she is not the stagnant warrior of regular armies, but is capable of changing with terrain and times. The guerrilla fighter.

As is true of all authentic subversives— the underground rebel, the elusive foot soldier—she always comes when needed, appearing in appropriate circumstances and dressed in such a way as to assure recognition, renew faith.

— Margaret Randall,
in *Guadalupe, Subversive Virgin*

The icon . . . represents a woman with dark skin and hair, her eyes downcast, in contrast to the straightforward gaze of Indian gods, and her hands raised before her in an Indian offertory gesture.

She wears a rose-colored shift filigreed in gold, and over it a cloak of blue-green, a color reserved for the chief god Omecihuatl, or Ome-Teotl, scattered with gold stars auguring a new age.

The black maternity band at her waist signals someone yet to come, and below it, over her womb, may appear the powerful Mesoamerican cross to suggest just how mighty this Someone will be.

The rays surrounding her form show her eclipsing the Sun Lord Tonatiuh; and the blackened crescent beneath her feet may be a phase of Venus, associated with Quetzalcoatl, the sacred plumed serpent . . .

She is borne by an intermediary "angel," the carrier of time and thus of a new era.

— Nancy Mairs,
in *Our Lady of Guadalupe and the Soup*

I don't want placed on my temple
the crown made from tinsel paper,
nor to play the pitiable role
of lunatic from Miramar.

I want on my modest altar
to bask in all the sweet warmth
of all those people who,
with love for me, and pleasure,
venerate that majestic flag
brandished by the liberator.

With a profane hand they desire
to turn me into a sovereign,
with scepter and royal tiara,
when I affirm as a motto
to be a Virgin of the Republic . . .

I went among the unlawful hordes
joining in the confrontation
and accompanied [them] in prison
giving hope and consolation . . .

I am the Virgin of Tepeyac
and I don't want to be a queen.
As Virgin I keep their respect
of my divine inspiration.

I will always be an amulet,
a candle that is not consumed,
and will be dressed in the feather
of that cherub that adores me.
I'll remain the humble lady
of Montezuma's native land.

I am the Virgin of the poor.
I don't want the monarchy!

— "El Hijo del Ahizote,"
1887 newspaper piece

Mary is the prophetic and liberating woman of the people . . . All the theological greatness of Mary is based on the lowliness of her historical condition.

Anticipating the liberating proclamation of her son, she shows herself attentive and sensitive to the fate of the humiliated and debased; in a context of praising God, she raises her voice in denunciation and invokes divine revolution in the relationship between oppressors and oppressed.

Mary loves the poor of Latin America. She took on the dark face of the slaves and the persecuted Amerindians . . . The masses of the poor bring their troubles to the centers of Marian pilgrimage; they dry their tears there and are filled with renewed strength and hope to carry on struggling and surviving.

— Leonardo and Clodovis Boff,
in *Liberation Theology*

Madre, you said, *is a holy word* . . .
Think of Our Lady . . .

When Juan Diego's cloak opened to the
    Catholic priests,
there she was: Nuestra Señora
    de Guadalupe, the
brown-skinned deliverer of the new raza.
    Her gift,
a batch of winter roses, borne on the cloth
of her own earth-fresh image.

— Alicia Gaspar de Alba,
in "Madre"

Invocation for Storing Corn

I myself
Spirit in Flesh:

come forth
elder sister
Lady of Our Flesh

soon I shall place you
inside my jade jar

hold up the four directions
don't shame yourself

you shall be my breath
you shall be my cure

for me, Poor Orphan
for me, Centeotl

you, my dear elder sister
you, Tonacacihuatl

— Traditional prayer,
translated by Francisco X. Alarcon

Could someone in my country by chance not
    love you,
beautiful sweet-smelling flower of the prairie?

. . . You even soften the rigors of the conquest.

Between the clouds of opal and amethyst
you show yourself to the Indian, calm
    his anguish,
and kiss and caress his despondent
    forehead too.

For you are like a gold lantern whose
    red-hot coals
help to keep the fire of our people blazing,
and with such tenderness you take into
    your hands
the heart and soul of each and every Mexican.

— Heriberto Barron

My grandmother did everything she could to turn her house in Los Angeles into one grand Mexican-Catholic altar.

There was the Last Supper in the dining room, of course, and little saintly medallions of the mail-order variety strategically placed in every room. A candle always burned before a gold-framed San Martin de Porres.

But it was *la Virgen* in the living room—by sheer size, the most important icon in the house—that fascinated me. Terrified me. Could save me. Was my mother. Was His mother. And was a virgin, but that didn't mean much to me; what mattered was that from her all things came: She was the Mother of God, the Goddess, the Witch, whatever you want to call her.

And best of all, she was *morena*: her olive skin, tinged with the glow of the omnipresent red light, was as dark as my own.

— Rubén Martinez,
in *The Undocumented Virgin*

Guadalupe chose to present Herself to the people as *la Morena,* a brown-skinned native woman, dressed in the robes of an Aztec princess.

She chose to appear to a humble corn farmer, "He who speaks like an eagle," Juan Diego, on a hillside, amid a choir of birds, in his native language.

There can be no doubt about who She is! She forced the Church, in spite of great resistance, to recognize Her.

And most importantly, she persists in the hearts of the people, holding together the very fabric of the culture, uniting them always.

— Luisah Teish,
in *The Warrior Queen: Encounters with a Latin Lady*

Juan Diego

An Indian's brown cheek
curved to a dusky rose,
Once long ago
upon Tepeyac's barren hill,
when winter roses bloomed
and roses were mere roses
in the glowing laughter
of the lady's smile.

My little son, I love you.

So all Tepeyac's holy hill
now sang an Indian lullaby
of roses and wild birds.

— Anne B. Quinn

This is the greatness of Mestizo culture, I think to myself. Everyone's welcome; we can all get along. Because of *Her*. Because She's both Indian and Spanish. A rocker and an Aztec dancer.

She's olive-skinned, a blend of indigenous copper brown and Iberian white. She's the woman that puts the Mexican macho in his place—no matter how much he beats his chest.

She's the origin of All Things, the serpent-woman, Tonantzin.

She is the protector of Family, and lashes out at anyone who would endanger a child's well-being. She is, after all, the Savior's Mother and sees Her Son's visage in the face of every Mexican son or daughter.

— Rubén Martinez,
in *The Undocumented Virgin*

There was a sighting a few years back of Her blurry image on the side of a modest stucco home in Watts, one of the many barrio destinations of the new immigrants in California. The TV news cameras didn't show much more than a curious play of shadow and light from a tree and the glow of a streetlamp, but thousands of faithful made the pilgrimage anyway.

In a small central California town, home to thousands of migrant workers, a statue of *la Virgen* inexplicably shed tears.

There is talk of a *Virgencita* luring border patrol guards down dead-end paths while the illegals cruise toward the American Dream on the other side of the arroyo.

I even heard a rumor that *la Virgen*'s serene countenance appeared before a crowd of hungover homeboys in Montbello, quivering in a big bowl of menudo.

It's no coincidence that She's been appearing more often lately. In times of crisis, She's always there. Today, the crisis is on both sides of the border.

— Rubén Martinez,
in *The Undocumented Virgin*

ᑽ Watch Out ᑽ

She's trouble. There's the time when Juan
Just wanted a quiet life and then one day,
Out of nowhere: flowers and song and on
The winter hill this beautiful woman, ok?

And this poor Juan, she says, has to go
To the bishop. He just wants to do his chores.
That is how she works. She's trouble, so:
If you see her, for you there's trouble in store.

— David Denny

La Raza

From the hill of Tepayac to the barrios of Los Angeles, the people carry you in their hearts, sweet Virgin of Guadalupe. Tucked into tiny shrines on remote Andean hillsides, tattooed on the arms of reformed gang members in Albuquerque, and plastered on the walls of every cantina in Latin America, you, Guadalupe, carry us.

The dark-skinned members of the Human Family, Guadalupe, have been trampled by the stampede of the American Dream. Mother of the Americas, you lift us, dust us off with your gentle hand, wipe our tears with your own lips, breathe your kindness back into our embittered lungs. With you looking over us, we can take the next step. We can walk all the way home.

You do not resemble the presidents of the United States of America, or the CEOs of global banks. You look like the *gardeners who trim the White House rose bushes, Madre Mia. You look like the nanny who puts the executive's children to bed. You look like our grandmothers looked when they were young novias getting ready for their bodas. You look like us.*

Virgen Maria de Guadalupe, you have evolved beyond Mary-meek-and-mild. You are ferocious. In the face of persecution, you rise like a lioness and roar; the pharaohs tremble before you. When life grows dull, you hang onto the waists of cute boys as they race down the highways on fast bikes, the wind in your mantle, miraculous roses blowing in a trail behind you.

You love blue corn atole, Madre Mia, and the beat of the ceremonial drum. You love tight jeans and black lace, mariachi music and fields of alfalfa flooded with irrigation waters. You love your children, whether they are fingering their rosaries or watching TV, when they are on their knees at your altar, weeping, and when they are melting into their first kiss. You love the poor and the broken, the clever and the simple, the criminal and the martyr. You love those who betrayed your firstborn Son.

Queridisima Guadalupe, how can we feel sorry for ourselves in light of your wild embrace of All That Is?

Closing Prayer

O, Our Lady of Guadalupe,
please grant me the grace
to keep the faith
when life makes no sense anymore.
Where once I dipped my bucket
effortlessly into the well of sweetness,
now I drink from the cup of bitterness.
You are an incarnation of Mother Mary.
You know what it is to experience
unbearable anguish,
and you radiate compassion to all
    who suffer,
pouring your unconditional love
into their shattered hearts.

O, Divine Mother,
look upon this broken world
with your healing gaze.
Make of your mercy
a salve in the palm of your Holy Hand
and press it into my own eyes,
banishing the darkness that has crept in

and clouded my vision.
Let me see clearly,
with hope and with joy,
once again.

Sweet Virgin of Tepeyac,
I am too often plagued
by frustration and impatience.
I tend to treat those I love most
with the least respect.
I find it difficult to accept the changes
unfolding in my life:
deaths and divorces,
untimely endings and
    unexpected beginnings.
I can rarely rise above
the quagmire of my own thoughts.
Please, *Madre Mia*, lift me out of myself.

Mother of All Peoples,
five hundred years ago
You appeared to an indigenous people
that had been decimated
by *conquistadores*.
They did not know where to turn.

Their Goddess had been overthrown
and their prayers had been viciously torn
from their tongues.
You came wearing the brown skin
of their own tribe.
You spoke to them in their native Nahuatl.
You promised them comfort
in their sorrowing
and protection from evil.
They have never stopped turning to you,
and you have never stopped
>   enfolding them
in your protective blanket.

Virgin of Guadalupe,
instill in me
the same joyous submission
that arose in the heart
of the gentle Juan Diego
when you came to him and gave him
your impossible command.
He hesitated.
You insisted.
And he surrendered,

dedicating himself wholly
to serving your divine will.
Help me to use him as a role model
and design my life around the glory
    of God,
rather than my own fleeting desires
And ephemeral fears.

Liberating Mother,
free me from slavery
to my own negative habits,
that I might be of service
in this suffering world.
Fill me with the courage
to stand up for the oppressed,
and the tenderness to forgive
the oppressors.
Give me the power
of strong convictions
and the flexibility
of an open mind.
Take the sword from my hand
and replace it with a basket of bread
for the hungry.

Show me the path of nonviolence.

O, Mystical Rose,
shower me today with your
miraculous blessings.
let me breathe the perfume of
    your blossoms
in the deep winter of my soul.

Amen.

— Mirabai Starr

Closing Prayer

Sources

Page 22-24:	"Hail, O Empress of America" from *Guadalupe*
Page 25:	"He was looking . . ." from *Guadalupe*
Page 26-27:	"When he stood . . ." from *Guadalupe*
Page 27-28:	"A great sign . . ." from *Guadalupe*
Page 29:	"As he neared . . ." from *Guadalupe*
Page 30-31:	*"Juan Diego:"* from *The Four Apparitions of Guadalupe*
Page 32-33:	"'I beg of you . . .'" from *Guadalupe*
Page 33-34:	"It is you . . ." from *The Four Apparitions of Guadalupe*
Page 34-35:	"And the Celestial Queen . . ." from *Guadalupe*
Page 36:	*"Juan Diego addresses the Archbishop: . . ."* from *The Four Apparitions of Guadalupe*
Page 37-38:	"Holy Flower of God" from *The Wonder of Guadalupe*

Page 39-40:	"Moon of the . . ." from *Guadalupe*
Page 41:	"Heavenly Protectress" from *Guadalupe*
Page 42:	"Only With You" from www.interlupe.com.mx
Page 43:	"Mary, Virgin of Guadalupe" from http://campus.udayton.edu/mary/resources/poetry
Page 52:	"Here I will hear . . ." from *The Wonder of Guadalupe*
Page 53-55:	"Our Lady of Guadalupe" from *Fire Above, Water Below*
Page 56-57:	"'Am I not here . . .'" from http://campus.udayton.edu/mary/resources/poetry
Page 57-58:	"To Our Lady Dark Yet Fair" from www.wf-f.org/guadalupe
Page 64-65:	"Know and be assured . . ." from *Guadalupe*
Page 66:	"Ave Maria" from www.interlupe.com.mx
Page 68:	"The Favor of Guadalupe" from www.interlupe.com.mx
Page 71-72:	"Face to Face" from www.interlupe.com.mx

Page 72-73:	"Definition" from www.interlupe.com.mx
Page 77:	*"Guadalupe to Juan Diego: . . ."* from *The Four Apparitions of Guadalupe*
Page 86-87:	"Known as Tonantzin . . ." from *Forgive Me, Mother, for My Crazy Life*
Page 88:	"Our Lady of Guadalupe . . ." from *Guadalupe, Subversive Virgin*
Page 89:	"The icon . . ." from *Our Lady of Guadalupe and the Soup*
Page 90-91:	"I don't want placed . . ." from *Guadalupe*
Page 92:	"Mary is the prophetic . . ." from *The Philosophical Quest*
Page 93:	*"Madre,* you said . . ." from *Three Times A Woman*
Page 94:	"Invocation for Storing Corn" from *Women In Praise of the Sacred*
Page 95:	"Could someone in . . ." from *Guadalupe*
Page 96:	"My grandmother did everything . . ." from *The Undocumented Virgin*

Page 97:	"Guadalupe chose to present..." from *The Warrior Queen: Encounters with a Latin Lady*
Page 98:	"Juan Diego" from http://campus.udayton.edu/mary/resources/poetry
Page 99:	"This is the greatness..." from *The Undocumented Virgin*
Page 100-101:	"There was a sighting..." from *The Undocumented Virgin*
Page 101:	"Watch Out" by Father David Denny (unpublished)

Bibliography

Books

Boff, Leonardo and Clodovis Boff. *Introducing Liberation Theology.* Maryknoll, NY: Orbis Books, 1987.

Castillo, Ana. *Goddess of the Amercias.* New York: Riverhead Trade, 1997.

Gaspar de Alba, Alicia, Maria Herrera-Sobek and Demetria Martinez. *Three Times a Woman: Chicana Poetry.* Tempe, AZ: Bilingual Press, 1989.

Johnston, Francis. *The Wonder of Guadalupe.* Rockford, IL: Tan Books, 1981.

McNichols, William Hart. *Fire Above, Water Below.* Unpublished.

Torres, Larry. *The Four Apparitions of Guadalupe.* Unpublished.

Zarebska, Carla. *Guadalupe.* Mexico: Equipar S. A. de C. V., 2002.

Websites

http://www.interlupe.com.mx

http://campus.udayton.edu/mary/resources/poetry

http://www.wf-f.org/guadalupe

Credits

Text Credits

"Our Lady of Guadalupe" in *Fire Above, Water Below* by Father William Hart McNichols used by permission of Father William Hart McNichols.

Excerpts by Luis J. Rodriguez from *Forgive Me, Mother, For My Crazy Life.* © 1996 by Luis J. Rodriguez. First published in *Goddess of the Americas/La Diosa de Las Americas: Writings on the Virgin de Guadalupe,* edited by Ana Castillo and published by Riverhead Books, New York. Reprinted by permission of Susan Bergholz Literary Services, New York and Lamy, NM. All rights reserved.

Excerpts by Rubén Martinez from *The Undocumented Virgin.* © 1996 by Rubén Martinez. First published in *Goddess of the Americas/La Diosa de Las Americas: Writings on the Virgin de Guadalupe,* edited by Ana Castillo and published by Riverhead Books, New York. Reprinted by permission of Susan Bergholz Literary Services, New York and Lamy, NM. All rights reserved.

Excerpt by Margaret Randall © 1996 Margaret Randall, "Guadalupe: The Subversive Virgin" reprinted with her permission.

Excerpts from *The Four Apparitions of Guadalupe* reprinted by permission of Larry Torres.

Excerpt from *Introducing Liberation Theology* reprinted by permission of Orbis Books.

Excerpts from *The Wonder of Guadalupe* reprinted by permission of Tan Books and Publishers.

"Madre," in Alicia Gaspar de Alba's collection "Beggar on the Cordoba Bridge" in *Three Times a Woman: Chicana Poetry* (Bilingual Press, 1989), reprinted with her permission.

Every effort has been made to contact the license holders for the excerpt by Nancy Mairs from "Our Lady of Guadalupe and the Soup" in *A Tremor of Bliss: Contemporary Writers on the Saints* edited by Paul Elie, the excerpt by Luisah Teish from "The Warrior Queen: Encounters with a Latin Lady," the excerpt from *Women in Praise of the Sacred* by Jane Hirshfield, and excerpts from *Guadalupe* by Carla Zarebska. Any questions about permissions should be directed to the permissions department at Sounds True: 413 S. Arthur Ave., Louisville, CO 80027.

Art Credits

Cover/Page xii:	Painting, Our Lady of Guadalupe, Photo © Beren Patterson / Alamy
Page xiv:	Photo, Our Lady of Guadalupe, © Todd Pierson / Alamy
Page 18:	Statue. Photo © Erika Walsh / Fotolia.com
Page 48:	Mosaic, Our Lady of Guadalupe, The National Shrine of the Immaculate Conception, Washington DC. Photo © William S. Kuta / Alamy
Page 82:	Photo, Car with Guadalupe. © Laroach / Dreamstime.com
Page 106:	Mural, Our Lady of Guadalupe, Chicago. Photo © Kim Karpeles / Alamy

About Sounds True

Sounds True was founded in 1985 with a clear vision: to disseminate spiritual wisdom. Located in Boulder, Colorado, Sounds True publishes teaching programs that are designed to educate, uplift, and inspire. We work with many of the leading spiritual teachers, thinkers, healers, and visionary artists of our time.

To receive a free catalog of tools and teachings for personal and spiritual transformation, please visit www.soundstrue.com, call toll-free 800-333-9185, or write to us at the address below.

SOUNDS TRUE
PO BOX 8010 / BOULDER, CO 80306